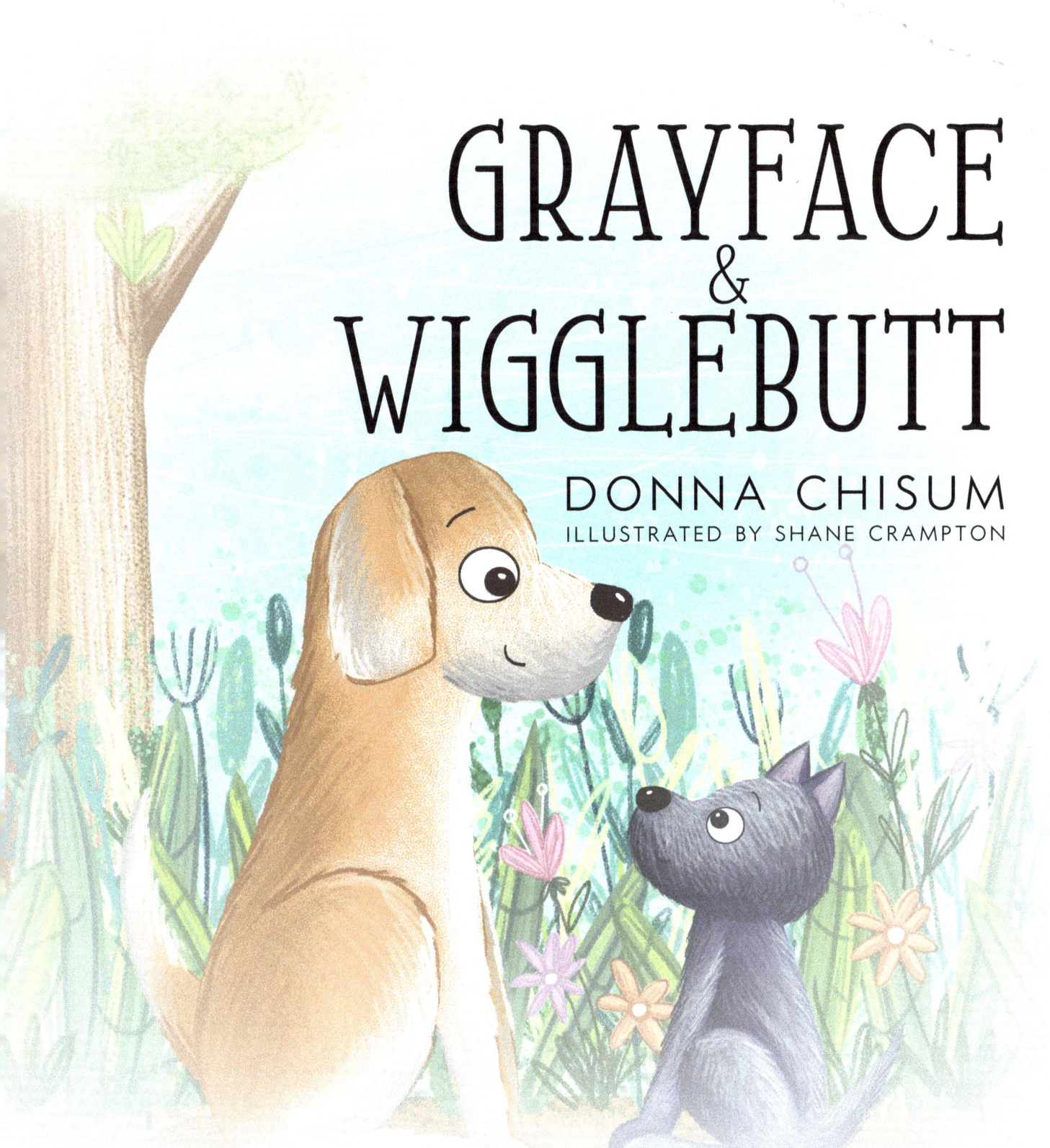

Copyright © 2023 by Donna Chisum. All rights reserved.
This book may not be reproduced or stored in whole or in part
by any means without the written permission of the author
except for brief quotations for the purpose of review.

ISBN: 978-1-960146-65-6 (hard cover)
978-1-960146-66-3 (soft cover)

Edited by: Amy Ashby

Published by Warren Publishing
Charlotte, NC
www.warrenpublishing.net
Printed in the United States

To Sylvia, whose kindness to a stranger
helped a lifelong dream come true.

Grayface and Wigglebutt were inseparable DBFs (doggie best friends) and lived on a farm with many acres to run and play and work. Grayface was aging, and his butterscotch fur was turning white, from his cold, wet nose to the very tip of his tail. Even his feet were white!

Wigglebutt was younger, with a thick coat of blackish-blue fur. Though not a puppy anymore, he was still excitable and barked at everything—mostly his imagination. When he was happy, his whole body wiggled, from his cold, wet nose to the very tip of his tail!

Summer workdays were long and hot and stinky for the DBFs. They scratched and pawed and helped their farmer dad spread hay for the horses.

They herded the cows back when they wandered too far away, and chased the chickens just to hear them squawk!

SQUAWK

The creek was their favorite place to cool off, and they jumped and splashed and showered anyone who got too close.

At bedtime, after their whirlwind days, they curled up together on soft blankets, and Grayface's snores echoed throughout the house.

One morning Grayface wouldn't get up, no matter how much Wigglebutt prodded and headbutted him. Their farmer mom called the doggie doctor—a veterinarian—to come to the farm.

The vet said Grayface was simply tired and that he expected the old dog would feel better the next day—and he was right, but Wigglebutt noticed Grayface couldn't run as fast as he used to, nor as far, and the old dog needed more days to rest between their adventures.

Grayface didn't want to play in the snow or run behind the tractor very often anymore, and Wigglebutt knew in his doggie heart that soon Grayface would chase his last squirrel.

When his final day came, Grayface's humans buried him under the tree he and Wigglebutt had peed on all the time (that's how the humans knew it was special). Wigglebutt lay at the grave every day, reminiscing about teasing the snapping turtle, chasing the chickens, and rolling in creek mud.

Wigglebutt's family told him all dogs go to heaven and that Grayface was as happy as a puppy again, but Wigglebutt was still heartbroken. The young dog no longer woofed when the wind blew or barked at every noise. Sometimes he wouldn't even eat! His family knew they had to find him another DBF soon.

One sunny spring afternoon as Wigglebutt lay sleeping on the porch, he heard a soft yip, and something jumped on his head!

He growled and yipped back at the creature and glared his most ferocious glare, but the new puppy was not afraid of him at all!

Day after day, Splotches, named because of his multicolored fur, nipped and bulldozed Wigglebutt to play. Wigglebutt wouldn't budge from his warm spot on the porch, but he was a tiny bit curious and kept a watchful eye on Splotches while pretending to sleep.

Many times, Wigglebutt felt his legs twitching as he imagined running through the fields again, but he was afraid; he didn't want to forget Grayface.

Eventually Wigglebutt couldn't resist and jumped up and chased Splotches off the porch! Splotches liked the game and kept pouncing and ramming into Wigglebutt until they were running just as Wigglebutt used to run with Grayface.

Wigglebutt told Splotches about his old friend. As he shared stories, he was relieved to realize he hadn't forgotten Grayface at all.

He also noticed how Splotches gnawed and chewed at his neck like Wigglebutt always had to Grayface.

And, just like Grayface had done to him, he sometimes had to growl Splotches away in order to get a little peace.

Although he was just six years old, Wigglebutt was now the "old man" dog.

He knew he had much to teach Splotches before the day when he would join Grayface under the tree, and he understood that although he missed his old friend, it was okay—and necessary—to make a new friend.

He woofed a challenge at Splotches to race for the barn, and the doggie hurricane whirled into new adventures!